SAM MITCHELL
WALLY SZCZERBIAK
CHRISTIAN LAETTNER
CHUCK PERSON
TERRELL BRANDON
ISAIAH RIDER
TONY CAMPBELL
TOM GUGLIOTTA
DOUG WEST
KEVIN GARNETT
TYRONE CORBIN
STEPHON MARBURY

THE HISTORY OF THE MINNESOTA TIMBERWOLVES

CREATIVE EDUCATION
JOHN NICHOLS

Published by Creative Education, 123 South Broad Street, Mankato, MN 56001

Creative Education is an imprint of The Creative Company.

Designed by Rita Marshall

Photos by Allsport, Rich Kane, NBA Photos, SportsChrome

Copyright © 2002 Creative Education. International copyright reserved in all countries.

No part of this book may be reproduced in any form

without written permission from the publisher.

Library of Congress Cataloging-in-Publication Data

Nichols, John, 1966- The history of the Minnesota Timberwolves / by John Nichols.

p. cm. – (Pro basketball today)   ISBN 1-58341-105-4

1. Minnesota Timberwolves (Basketball team)–

Juvenile literature. [1. Minnesota Timberwolves (Basketball team)–History.

2. Basketball–History.] I. Title. II. Series.

GV885.52.M565 N52 2001   796.323'64'09776579–dc21   00-047329

First Edition 9 8 7 6 5 4 3 2 1

MINNEAPOLIS AND SAINT PAUL

ARE KNOWN AS MINNESOTA'S

"TWIN CITIES." DIVIDED BY THE MIGHTY MISSISSIPPI RIVER,

the two communities—and towns throughout Minnesota—share a love for recreation in the great outdoors. Whether camping, boating, or fishing, people in the "Land of 10,000 Lakes" enjoy being out among the elements.

On moonlit nights, the lonesome howl of one of Minnesota's defining animals can sometimes be heard echoing through the state's northern forests. The secretive timberwolf roams many of the same woods as Minnesota's outdoor adventurers. In 1989, when the National Basketball Association (NBA) granted Minnesota a new team, it seemed

SIDNEY LOWE

only natural to name the franchise in honor of the state's best-known predators—the Timberwolves.

In statewide voting, "Timberwolves" beat out "Polars" as the name of the new franchise.

{MUSSELMAN ANSWERS THE CALL} As an expansion team, Minnesota's first roster was made up primarily of players that other teams didn't want and had released. So, when the Timberwolves looked for their first coach, they wanted someone who could squeeze the maximum amount of effort out of each player. The man they found for the job was Bill Musselman.

Musselman led the University of Minnesota to a Big 10 Conference championship in the 1970s and had gone on to coach at all levels of professional basketball. His trademark was intensity, and his ability to motivate players was well-known. "It's great to be here," Musselman said in his characteristically blunt style. "Now let's build a winner."

KEVIN GARNETT

Tyrone Corbin worked the boards hard in Minnesota's first two seasons.

TYRONE CORBIN

Building a winner would not be easy for Musselman, as the Timberwolves had little talent. Still, the team did feature some players who shared their coach's affinity for hard work, physical play, and stubborn defense. These players included guards Sidney Lowe and Tony Campbell, forwards Sam Mitchell and Tod Murphy, and center Brad Lohaus.

The Wolves earned their first victory as Campbell poured in 38 points and key reserve forward Tyrone Corbin grabbed 13 rebounds in a 125–118 win over the Philadelphia 76ers. Victories were scarce for Minnesota in 1989–90, but the team was a hit at the ticket office. Playing in the Metrodome that first season, the Timberwolves drew an NBA-record 1,072,572 fans over the course of the year.

The next season, after the team moved into the brand-new Target Center, Minnesota's younger players began to improve. Point guard

| Tony Campbell paced the first-year Wolves in scoring, pouring in 23 points a game.

TONY CAMPBELL

Center Dean Garrett was a rugged rebounder and intense low-post defender.

DEAN GARRETT

Jerome "Pooh" Richardson became a starter and added spark to Minnesota's attack. The Wolves improved to 29–53, but trouble brewed within the organization. The team's front office wanted Musselman to develop younger players such as Richardson and rookie center Felton Spencer, while the coach wanted to play his proven veterans. With the two sides unable to work out their differences, Musselman resigned after the 1990–91 season.

Young point guard Pooh Richardson's 734 assists in **1990–91** *set a long-standing team record.*

{LAETTNER BRINGS HOPE} After Musselman's departure, the Timberwolves brought in former Boston Celtics coach Jimmy Rodgers to lead the team. Unfortunately, with Rodgers at the helm, the Timberwolves took a step back, posting a miserable 15–67 record in 1991–92. One of the biggest obstacles to the team's development was its bad luck in the NBA Draft. Despite posting poor records their first two

CHRISTIAN LAETTNER

seasons, the Timberwolves were never able to draft high enough to land an impact player to turn things around.

In 1992, the Wolves used the third overall pick—their highest ever—

to choose Duke University center Christian Laettner. The 6-foot-11 and 240-pound Laettner had excelled at Duke with a variety of skills. A strong rebounder, Laettner was also a solid ball handler and had an accurate shooting stroke. "Christian gives Minnesota their first star quality guy," said Laettner's college coach, Mike Krzyzewski.

> The 1992–93 Wolves team set franchise records with a 32-point win and a 37-point loss.

The Wolves also made a key trade, sending Richardson and Mitchell to the Indiana Pacers for sharpshooting forward Chuck "the Rifleman" Person and point guard Michael Williams. Despite the additions, the Timberwolves remained at the bottom of the Midwest Division, and Rodgers was fired as head coach.

{WOEFUL WOLVES} To replace Rodgers, the Wolves turned to Sidney Lowe, the team's former point guard. With Lowe leading the way, the Timberwolves put forth a stronger effort, but the losses continued to pile up. Minnesota won only 19 games in 1992–93 and 20 the following year. Except for Laettner and shooting guard Isaiah Rider, the team's top pick in the 1993 NBA Draft, the Timberwolves' roster con-

ISAIAH RIDER

sisted mostly of journeymen and aging veterans.

Forced to carry the franchise at such young ages, Laettner and Rider struggled under the pressure. Rider was an explosive scorer, but he was

also wildly inconsistent in both his play and behavior. He often followed strong performances with poor ones and repeatedly ran into trouble on and off the court. Laettner, meanwhile, grew frustrated by the team's struggles. "The losing just turns you numb after a while," he said. "I lost more games here in a month than I did my whole college career."

Although the Wolves' young duo struggled at times, they also gave the team its best chance to win. Laettner and Rider combined to average more than 33 points and 12 rebounds a game in 1993–94. Rider also thrilled Wolves fans by winning the 1994 Slam-Dunk Contest during the All-Star Game weekend held in Minneapolis.

During the 1994–95 season, the Timberwolves' erratic play nearly led the team to be sold to a group that wanted to move it to New Orleans. Fortunately for supportive Minnesota fans, the NBA vetoed the sale, and the team was instead sold to local businessman Glen Taylor.

The first move made under the new owner was replacing Lowe as head coach with Bill Blair. Coach Blair tried desperately to bring new

Veteran forward Thurl Bailey was a key reserve post player for the Wolves in the early **'90s**.

THURL BAILEY

Like Christian Laettner, forward LaPhonso Ellis was known for his great versatility.

life to the team, but the Wolves' weak offense and rebounding doomed his efforts. The one bright spot of an otherwise dismal 1994–95 season was a trade that sent disappointing young forward Donyell Marshall to the Golden State Warriors for 6-foot-10 power forward Tom Gugliotta. Gugliotta's inside strength gave the team a big boost, but it couldn't save Minnesota from setting an NBA record with a fourth straight season of at least 60 losses.

> Guard Terry Porter helped Minnesota lead the NBA in free throw accuracy in **1995–96**.

{GARNETT—THE TEEN WOLF} In 1995, the Timberwolves' front office was rebuilt, and former Boston Celtics star and Minnesota native Kevin McHale took over the team's basketball operations. McHale had won two NBA championships with the Celtics, and he hoped to breathe life into the luckless Timberwolves. "We're officially out of excuses," McHale said. "Our fans have been patient. Now we have

TERRY PORTER

to give them something to get excited about."

McHale knew it would take bold moves to turn the Wolves around, and he made one by selecting high school phenom Kevin

Garnett with the fifth overall pick in the 1995 NBA Draft. Most NBA scouts thought that the 6-foot-11 Garnett was destined for stardom . . . someday. But at age 19 and with no college experience, many feared that

the youngster was not ready for the professional ranks.

When he signed with the Wolves, Garnett became only the fourth player ever to jump straight from high school to the NBA. Tall, agile, and fiercely competitive, Garnett appeared to be the impact player the Wolves hungered for, but many fans wondered if the team would be patient enough to let his raw talent develop.

Fortunately, Garnett found an immediate mentor in McHale. The former All-Star forward spent hours on the court working with Garnett to improve his game. To ensure that Garnett was allowed to develop at his own pace, the Wolves hired McHale's good friend and former college teammate Phil "Flip" Saunders as the team's new head coach. McHale and Saunders shared a common vision of what needed to be done to make the Wolves a contender.

Guard James Robinson scored a team-record 23 points in one quarter of a game in **1996–97**.

JAMES ROBINSON

Sam Mitchell gave the Wolves savvy leadership throughout the **1990s**.

SAM MITCHELL

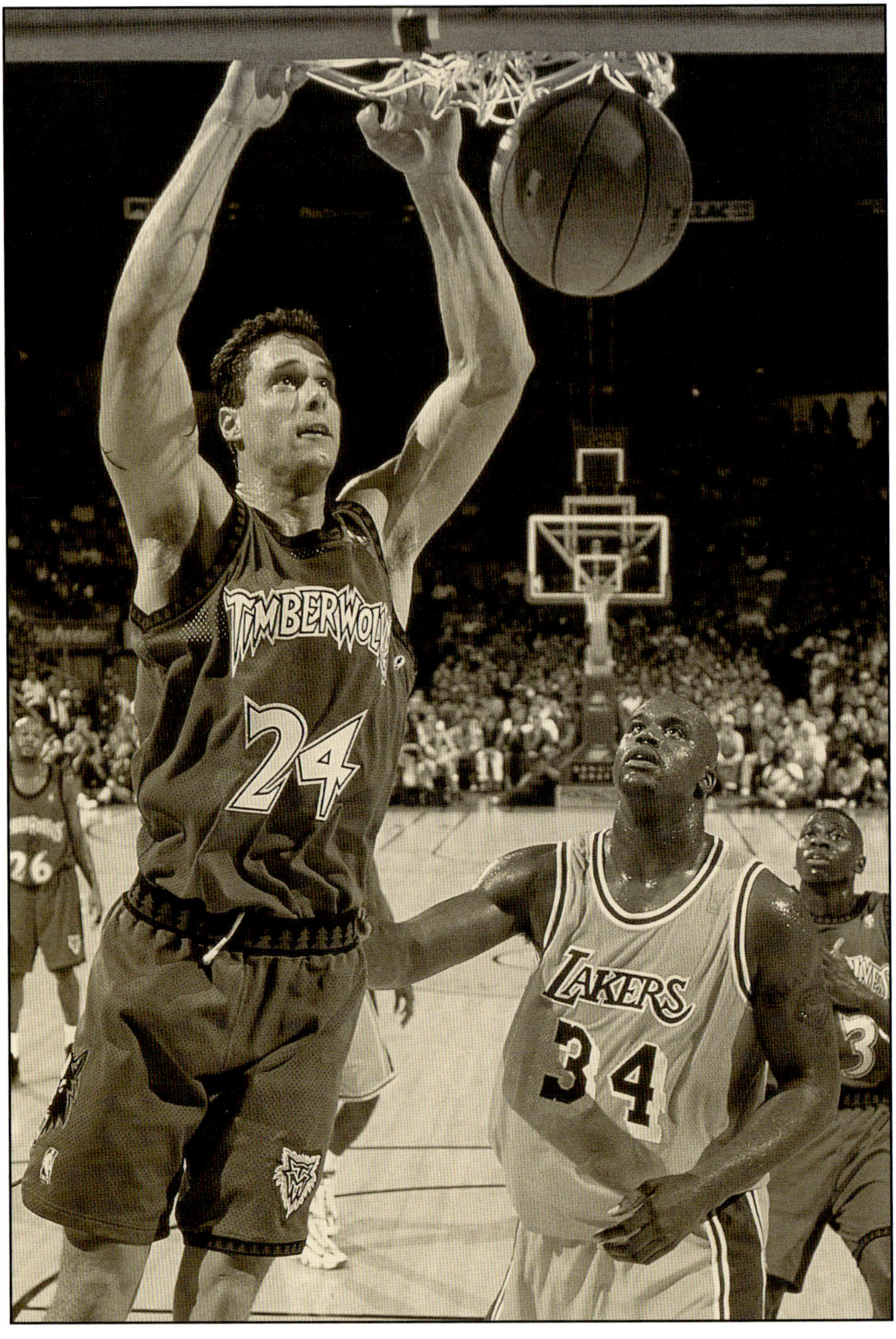
TIMBERWOLVES
24
26
LAKERS
34

In 1995–96, under Saunders's guidance, the team broke its streak of 60-loss seasons by going 26–56. Midway through the year, an unhappy Laettner was shipped to the Atlanta Hawks, opening significant playing time for Garnett. The rookie proved more than willing to be the team's go-to player, a role the charismatic young star seemed born to play.

{PLAYOFFS AT LAST} After enduring seven long years of futility, Minnesota fans enjoyed their first taste of postseason basketball in 1996–97. That season, the Timberwolves jumped to 40–42 and made the playoffs as Garnett blossomed in his role as a team leader. The young forward averaged 17 points, 8 rebounds, and 2 blocked shots per game. "That kid is the future of basketball," said Houston Rockets forward Charles Barkley. "He says he's 6-foot-11, but he's a 7-footer who can run, jump, and play all three of the frontcourt positions."

In **1997**, forward Tom Gugliotta was the first Minnesota player named to an NBA All-Star Game.

TOM GUGLIOTTA

The 1996–97 Wolves also featured a new weapon in Stephon Marbury, a point guard from Georgia Tech taken in the first round of the 1996 NBA Draft. The lightning-quick Marbury teamed up with

Garnett to give the Wolves an explosive inside-outside attack.

"Sometimes I don't know whether to yell at them or spank them," quipped Coach Saunders. "It's tough to expect so much from guys so young, but they have really responded."

But Garnett and Marbury weren't the team's only talented players. Gugliotta netted 20 points per game, and hardworking center Dean Garrett and guard Doug West gave the team a pair of defensive stoppers. The young Wolves were quickly swept from the 1997 playoffs by the veteran Houston Rockets, but Minnesota was on its way up.

> As a rookie, point guard Stephon Marbury dished out nearly eight assists a game.

Heading into the 1997–98 season, the Timberwolves were ready to post their first winning record. The road was not easy, though. With Gugliotta and guard Chris Carr sidelined by injuries, Minnesota turned to veterans Terry Porter and Sam Mitchell (who had returned to the Wolves) to keep the team on track. Mitchell provided leadership and clutch shooting, while the 34-year-old Porter gave the Wolves a dependable ball handler at the point guard position.

STEPHON MARBURY

Even with the solid contributions of their veterans, the Wolves knew they would go only as far as their two young stars took them.

Marbury's relentless attacking style blended perfectly with Garnett's ability to run the floor and finish off fast breaks. Behind their efforts, the Wolves finished the regular season 45–37 and pushed the heavily favored Seattle SuperSonics to a deciding fifth game before bowing out in the first round of the playoffs.

> Sharpshooter Anthony Peeler hit 45 percent of his three-point bombs during the **1997–98** season.

{READY TO HOWL} After the Wolves' step forward in 1997–98, the team took a step back the next season. Just as Minnesota had begun to build around its core of Gugliotta, Garnett, and Marbury, Gugliotta left town as a free agent, and Marbury—a New York City native—demanded a trade to an East Coast city and was dealt to the New Jersey Nets.

Though the losses were devastating, the Wolves moved quickly to

ANTHONY PEELER

reload. They signed talented forward Joe Smith to replace Gugliotta and acquired All-Star point guard Terrell Brandon in the Marbury trade. Still, the new Wolves struggled in 1998–99. Garnett, Smith, and Brandon carried the team back into the postseason, but Minnesota fell to the eventual league champion San Antonio Spurs in the first round.

One of the reasons for the Timberwolves' early exits from the playoffs had been the team's lack of a reliable outside shooter. In 1999, Minnesota addressed that need by drafting sharpshooting forward Wally Szczerbiak. The 6-foot-8 and 245-pound forward was a dual threat, able to both light it up from three-point range and power his way inside. "Wally's a smart kid with a great work ethic," said Coach Saunders. "With his shooting, teams won't be able to gang up on Kevin as much anymore."

Forward Joe Smith gave the Wolves a formidable shot blocker in the late **1990s**.

JOE SMITH

Behind point guard Terrell Brandon, Minnesota led the NBA in assists in **1999–00**.

TERRELL BRANDON

Up-and-coming forward Wally Szczerbiak was a valuable scoring threat from anywhere on the court.

WALLY SZCZERBIAK

After also adding promising point guard William Avery in the same draft and signing free agent swingman Malik Sealy, the deeper, more balanced Timberwolves raced to their best record ever in 1999–00, going 50–32. Minnesota fell to the powerful Portland Trail Blazers in the playoffs, but it was dealt a harsher blow a few weeks later when Sealy was killed in a car accident. The Wolves were determined to honor their fallen teammate by continuing to improve in the seasons ahead.

In a little more than a decade, Minnesota fans have watched their team evolve from a league doormat to a contender. The steps along the way have sometimes been painful, but the tough times have helped narrow the focus of this rising young team. Winners at last, today's Timberwolves hope to soon let out a championship howl.

> Guard Chauncey Billups helped the Wolves win a club-record 11 straight games in **2000–01**.

CHAUNCEY BILLUPS